RIO

TEXT: **AARON COHEN**

1st. Edition, September 1978
I.S.B.N.
84-7424-020-4

GEOCOLOR® S.A.

THE CARIOCA

«Carioca is someone who came and stayed»
Billy Blanco
(samba composer born in Belém do Pará)

If this is your first time in Rio de Janeiro let me tell you something that the pretty pictures that you will see in this book won't be able to say about the people you are going to meet here, namely the Carioca, (anyone who was born in Brasil or anywhere in the world— even in Rio. The streets of this surprising city are full of them).

Let's begin with those who form the greater part of our people: waiters, porters, elevator-operators, laborers, samba dancers, or just the people that newspapers call the *masses,* the people who stand for hours on end on the sidewalk just watching, not an accident, but a bulldozer digging up the ground. Improvisation is their best skill and they can't refrain from doing something that they consider is good, completely sure that the outcome will be positive. And against all scientific laws and probabilities, they end up doing it fine, for as they say, God is Brazilian (more likely carioca) therefore being also able to improvise.

A carioca will call you by your first name the first time you meet, and by the second time he will be your childhood friend, patting you on the back affectionately and hugging you in the middle of the street, celebrating that wonderful event of two people meeting.

It is convenient to know that most appointments, dates and meetings are not pre-arranged, and people meet just because it happens and so they just show up when they feel like it. Pre-arranged meetings at a fixed time are a myth for the carioca and when they do fix one, there is always a very subtle loophole in their conversation with you which will indicate if they are going to appear or not.

And what conversation! They talk, argue, pull faces, elbow each other, tell jokes, laugh, suddenly call out to greet someone on the other side of the street, shut up when a good-looking woman walks by them, pass comments about her, and — back to their conversation. Nobody seems to listen to anyone; everybody is talking at the same time and roaring with laughter.

Withdrawing from all this noise you turn the next corner and will suddenly find yourself in a quiet street, with the hillside right over you and old houses covered with tiles that take you back to colonial times. If you walk up this narrow street, in a few moments you will find yourself surrounded by greenery, in the shade of huge trees with birds singing and butterflies playing.

From the top of the hill you will see the view open out at your feet offering you the whole city between the mountains and the ocean. After looking for a while you will feel the urge to get back downtown; back to the bustle of its streets and the exciting company of the cariocas.

By then— watch out!! you will be on the brink of staying in Rio for good and becoming Carioca as well.

FERNANDO SABINO

RIO DE JANEIRO

There are cities whose secrets can be told in few words. Others we are unable to imagine without the aid of pictures. We have to sketch their profiles and color them.
With Rio de Janeiro it is even more difficult. Its colors, profiles and smells are unique in the world. There is no way to describe such a wealth of sensations. Even the best photographers, most brilliant writers, and smartest film-makers have never been able to grasp and convey the magical beauty of Rio. All images seem faint and all adjectives sound gross when they are applied to this limitless city. The same happens with Rio as with that old wine-maker in Burgundy, who, after treating his guests to the best wines in his cellar, asked them to write their opinions in a book. He ended up having a unique collection of autographs of the most famous figures of our times: Churchill, Einstein, Toscanini, Freud, etc., who wrote the simplest remarks in that

SUNSET AT THE PÃO DE AÇUCAR (THE SUGAR LOAF)

PRAIA VERMELHA (RED BEACH)

SUGAR LOAF CABLE CAR

PÃO DE AZUCAR

GUANABARA MITOLOGICA
A 1ª ESTATUA DEDICADA
à GUANABARA MARAVILHOSA
REPRESENTADAS
NOS CABELOS, AS SUAS FLORESTAS,
NOS SEIOS, AS SUAS MONTANHAS,
NAS CURVAS DO BUSTO, AS SUAS PRAIAS,
NAS VOLUTAS, ATE A CINTURA,
AS ONDAS DO SEU MAR,
NA SILHUETA, ESBELTA A GRAÇA
DE SUA MULHER.

MONUMENT
TO ESTACIO
DE SA

COVE OF
BOTAFOGO

PÃO DE AZUCAR

MONUMENT
TO «LOS
PRACINHAS»
(BRAZILIAN
SOLDIERS
OF THE 2nd
WORLD WAR)

CORCOVADO

OUR LORD REDEEMER EMBRACING
GUANABARA

PALM-TREES ON THE WAY TO THE CORCOVADO
PEAK.

PICTURESQUE TRAIN UP THE CORCOVADO

album. A genius said: «It is a great wine». An inspired poet wrote: «There is nothing better than wine» and on another page a Nobel price winner said: «Hurrah for the wine!».

Those who visit Rio de Janeiro usually fail in their attempt to adorn with adjectives the most beautiful city in the world; when in 1552 Tomé de Sousa saw it for the first time, he said: «All in her is full of grace». A popular song calls her «the wonderful city», and Stephan Zweig modestly wrote, «the beauty of this city is unexplainable».

And this is the absolute truth.

HISTORY IN THE STREETS

Getting to know a city also implies learning the psicology of its inhabitants. We can get an idea of the carioca (Brazilian) soul by watching the life of Rio. In this city, history is not hidden in old parchments of dubious penmanship. There are nevertheless old chronicles that have recorded the life of the city over four centuries. But the true history of Rio is to be learned in the open air of its streets and squares, as well as in the barroque decoration of a facade and the contagious happynes of the «carioca» people.

Until the XVI century, this land around the Bay of Guanabara was the paradise of the tamoyo indians. The French and Portuguese fought over it until the latter gained control of the region. Rio was a poor city for many years, dedicated to the cultivation of sugar cane, and it was only in the XVIII century that it gained some importance as a port for exporting the gold just discovered in Minas Gerais. In 1763 it became the capital city of Brasil.

Since then, Rio has been the site of the key events of the country's history, such as the

CORCOVADO - VIEW OF THE CHRIST STATUE.

9

CORCOVADO - OBSERVATORY

GUANABARA BAY

PAIA VERMELHA, COPACABANA IN THE
CKGROUND

RIO DE JANEIRO

winning of Independence in 1822 and the proclamation of the Republic in 1889.
In recent times (1960), the capital was moved to Brasilia, and Rio was made the new State of Guanabara. In 1975 it became the capital of Rio de Janeiro State made of 64 smaller towns and with a population of 10 million people.
Its history is replayed before our eyes as we visit the old buildings: The Monastery of Sâo Bento, founded by the Benedictine monks in 1641; the imposing aqueduct of Los Arcos, built 200 years ago; the Viceroy's palace, a magnificent example of XVIII century carioca architecture; the Convent of San Antonio; the church of Our Lady do Outeiro da Gloria; the old houses in colonial style with their beautiful wrought iron balconies. Here and there, in the oldest parts of the city one can discover vestiges of Colonial times, which little by little are giving way to the modern skyscraper.
When the Court House was moved to Rio de Janeiro, the city became one of the most active

*HYDROFOILS CROSS GUANABARA BAY BETWEEN
RIO AND NITEROI*

DOWNTOWN
GRACA ARANHA AVENUE
PRESIDENTE VARGAS AVENUE

15th OF NOVEMBER SQUARE
FERRY-BOAT STATION AT THE 15th OF NOVEMBER SQUARE
POST OFFICE BUILDING - FORMER IMPERIAL PALACE.

THE MUNICIPAL THEATER

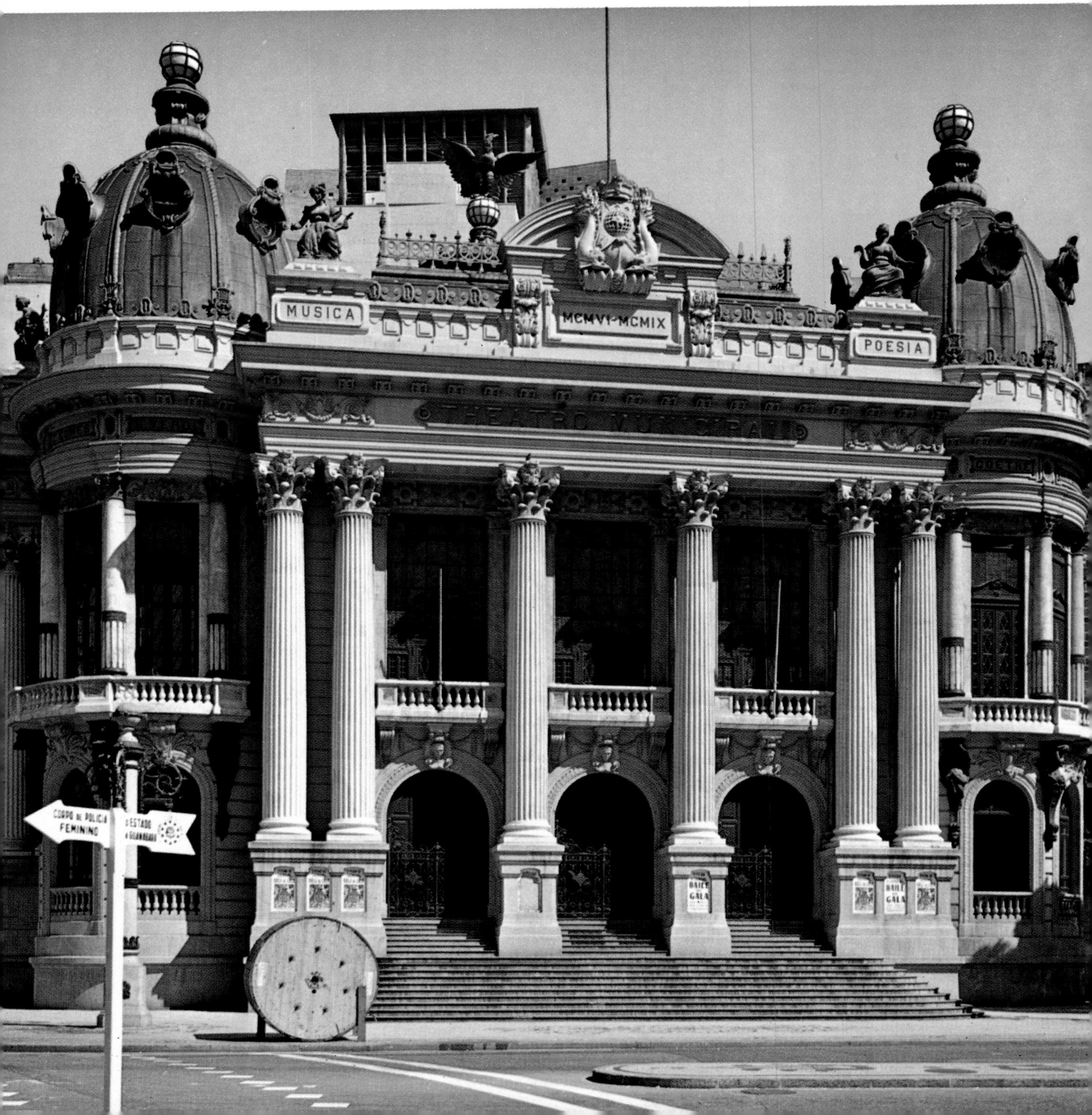

and advanced capitals of the time. Around that time the Mint was built, and other buildings like the Bank of Brasil, The National Press, the School of Fine Arts, the National Museum, and the Botanical Garden was created. In 1811 the Prince Don Juan attended the first mass to be held in the church of La Candelaria, the greatest and most barroque in the city.

All this historical heritage survives beside the most daring architecture of the XX century. The secret of Rio lies precisely in how gracefully it harmonizes its mixture of races, history and styles. Like the verdant landscape all around it, the city offers the traveller a surprise at every corner.

NATURE IS PART OF THE CITY

There are few cities in the world which can compete with Rio's privileged geographical situation. It is not just a city to be appreciated solely for its urban development. One needs to know its hills and beaches, lakes and gardens. On the warmest days in the year, when the tropical aromas are strongest and most penetrating, the live proximity of the jungle is clearly felt. Nature's presence almost reaches inside the buildings. Contrary to other modern cities, Rio is not a cement monster. Its skyscrapers seem to grow out from the beaches or from the parks full of flowers, just like the palm trees. The very breath of the earth is felt in its gardens.

Surrounded by the ocean, from the Bay of Guanabara to the beaches of Grumari and the Barra of Guaratiba, the city is divided in two well defined zones. It is to the south that the

LA CANDELARIA CHURCH

18

CHURCH OF THE MONASTERY OF SÃO BENTO

FACADE OF THE CHURCH OF THE SÃO BENTO MONASTERY

MARECHAL FLORIANO
SQUARE

NATIONAL LIBRARY
MUNICIPAL THEATER
CINELANDIA (MOVIE DISTRICT)

tourist attractions can be found: the best hotels and restaurants, the dazzling beach of Copacabana, the imposing peak of El Corcovado and the romantic forest of Tijuca.

THE BEACHES

The beaches of Rio are simply the most beautiful in the world, and also offer the opportunity to get to know in more detail the life and habits of its people. These beaches, while open to the classiest tourist, dotted with five star hotels, still welcome the common people from adjoining city neighborhoods. In Copacabana, Ipanema or Leblon, are to be found popular figures of carioca life, such as the fresh drink sellers, and vendors of straw hats and paper parrots. And at dawn one can still see fishermen dragging on the sand their catch up the beach.

During the first years of carioca history, when the governors built their houses on the heights above the city in search of a healthier climate, it was the poor people who lived by the ocean. Sea bathing started to become popular in the early XIX century. But the peak years of Copacabana and its vicinity came in the thirties. Then a real estate boom took place and the old mansions and summer villas were demolished in order to build the modern day skyscrapers. Today, the bars on the shore are crowded with happy, idle people looking for fun. Copacabana became a city in its own right in the heart of Rio. It is precisely in this strip of land between the mountains and the ocean that we can find all that a great city has to offer: the best stores, banks, hotels, nightclubs, restaurants, plus three miles of sandy beaches with the highest density per square yard of beautiful women in the world.

However, Copacabana is only one of the innumerable beaches in Rio, which include Flamengo, Botafogo, Urca, Ipanema, Leblon, Sâo Conrado, Praia de Barra, etc. Each one with its own belle epoque and its own tradition. Flamengo is today the most developed of these beaches and the nearest to the center of the city. Ipanema was the beach in vogue during the fifties and it was in one of its bohemian bars (El Veloso) that the *bossa nova,* the brasilian rhythm which conquered the world was born; Ipanema developed its own folklore

THE CARIOCA
AQUEDUCT

THE CARIOCA
AQUEDUCT.

TIRADENTES
SQUARE.

SAN FRANCISCO CHURCH

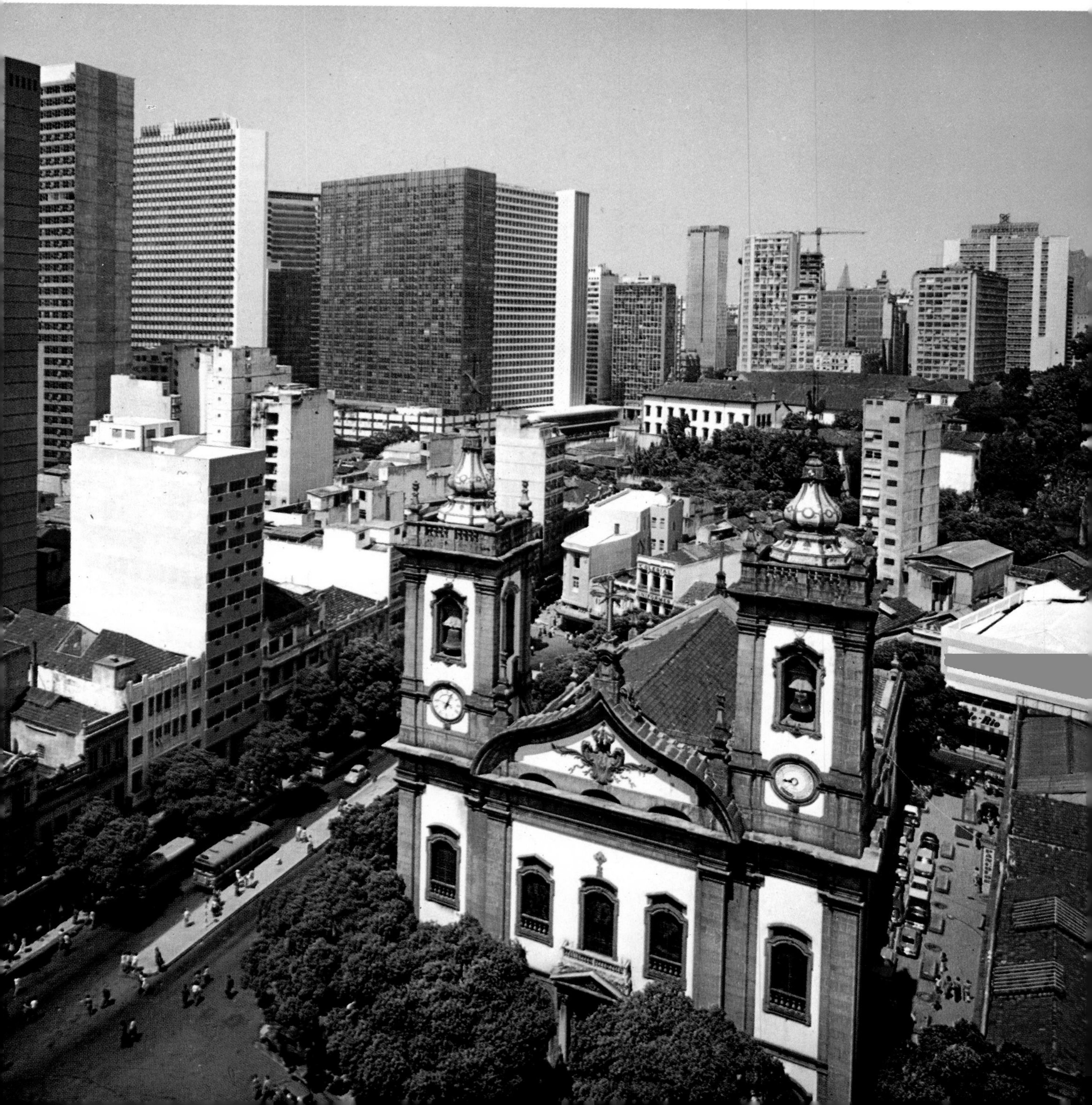

ARCHITECTURE CONTRASTS: THE OLD CONVENT OF
ST. ANTONIO IN FRONT OF THE METROPOLITAN
CATHEDRAL

NEW CATHEDRAL.

has been built. A little further to the south we find the longest beach in Rio, The Praia da Barra, which extends for almost 9 miles.
Year by year Rio's shoreline grows and is transformed at an incredible speed. This hectic, feverish city seeks rest in the cool ocean breeze of its beaches.

HILLS AND LANDSCAPES

Rio de Janeiro is a city sculpted in space. Its horizontal dimensions and its hills provide a unique vertical perpective. Within these two dimensions, the twisted city landscape stretches out like a barroque sculpture. To travel from one part of the city to another it is necessary to go through tunnels drilled under the mountains. Directly above these underground avenues and nesting humbly in their poverty the «favelas», (ghettos) have sprung up, home of the neediest of Rio's people. The favelas are not a problem belonging solely to Rio, for all big cities in the world know the same situation. Here, however, the poor, in contrast to what happens in other parts of the world, live in close contact with the sun and have not been placed in those distant suburbs where other large cities hide their poverty. Some of the mountains are grey and rugged and others gentle and green, and each part of the landscape is different. On the ocean side of the city uncountable islands reflect the sun and the other side is bounded by virgin jungle with its lush greenery. Winding through the midst of all this, the city, with its avenues and skyscrapers. Some of the best architects of our time have set their works in this spacial paradise: Oscar Niemeyer, Lúcio Costa, Maurício Roberto, Sérgio Bernades, Carlos Leâo, etc.
The peak of El Corcovado, with its monumental statue of Jesus Christ the Redeemer, rises up from the National park of Tijuca, the largest forest reserve of the city. The peak reaches 2.100 feet above sea level and delights our eyes with a matchless panorama. The summit is conquered by means of a picturesque train ride, passing through beautiful natural scenery. From

and even publishes a magazine: «O Pasquin» a joyful weekly which transformed the literary style of carioca journalism. We should not forget the famous «Banda de Ipanema», which today forms part of the musical tradition in the Carnival.
The beach of Leblon was the last to become fashionable, and many of its bars are already part of the bohemian history of Rio: Antonio's, Degrau, Luna Bar, and others.
Between Leblon and Sâo Conrado lies the quiet beach of Vidigal, where a huge tourist complex

THE NEW
CATHEDRAL
(INTERIOR)

MUSEUM OF
MODERN
ART
FAÇADE

MUSEUM OF
MODERN
ART
GARDENS

NATIONAL ART
MUSEUM.

the heights we can enjoy the entire Bay of Guanabara, Flamengo beach and the enormous bridge connecting Rio with Niteroi. To the other side the view offers the waters of the lake Rodrigo de Freitas and the distant beaches of Ipanema and Leblon.

The statue of Jesus Christ, with his arms opened as if protecting the city, is 110 feet high. Under its marble base is a small chapel in which a mass is said every sunday and has been ever since 1931, the year of its construction.

From «El Mirante Da Marta» there is also a magnificent view to be admired over the Park of Tijuca and the pretty cove of Botafogo.

But, despite all these attractions, the place most visited by travelers coming to Rio is without any doubt the peak called Pan de Azucar (the sugar loaf), an international symbol portrayed on all tourist posters, being to Rio what the Eiffel tower is to Paris or Big Ben to

BRAZILIAN HISTORY - COVER OF THE GOLD-EMBOSSED VELVET BINDING OF THE ORIGINAL EDITION OF THE FIRST BRAZILIAN CONSTI-TUTION (1824) NATIONAL ARCHIVE OF RIO DE JANEIRO

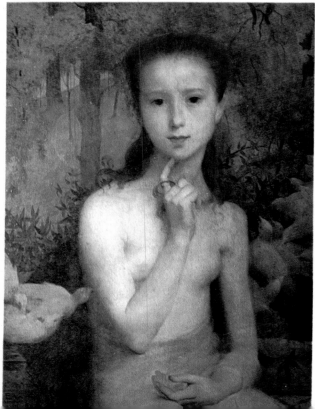

London. The climb of 1.200 feet is easily accomplished using the suspended cable car; the sight is overwhelming, for one can admire all the coastline of Rio, with its bays and coves: at night the city shines like a diamond. Besides Pan de Azúcar and El Corcovado, there are other places offering beautiful views of the city — Vista Chinesa, the peak of Urca and Mesa do Imperador (Emperors table), natural terraces placed between the deep blue of the sky and the ocean.

THE MUSEUMS

Rio is not just the most beautiful spectacle in the world. It is also a city of cultural traditions that have been preserved together with its social and political history. The greater part of

FLAMENGO PARK AT NIGHT

COPACABANA BEACH

COPACABANA BEACH ·FISHERMEN

COPACABANA STREET FAIR FLOWERS
TROPICAL FRUITS

this patrimony is kept in museums, some of them installed in great mansions and palaces that well deserve a visit in their own right. The National Museum, founded by Don João VI is the oldest scientific institution in the country. Gathered under its roof are more than a million samples of Zoology, Archaeology, Mineralogy, Ethnography, etc. One of the most striking pieces is the Bendegó meteorite, weighing more than *five tons,* the largest meteorite ever to fall on the Southern Hemisphere. The National Museum is placed in a magnificent XIX century building, La Quinta de Boa Vista, (The country house of the nice view), which was the seat of two successive governments before the proclamation of the Republic in 1889. In its halls the first Brasilian Constitutional Assembly was held in 1891.

A visit to the History Museum is of special interest. Founded in 1922, and placed in the old

IPANEMA BEACH

PRAIA DE IPANEMA - PRATICA DE SURF   *IPANEMA BEACH*

fortress of São Tiago, this was an old slave prison, and also arsenal and home of the Royal Military Academy.
The Museum preserves a valuable collection of documents about the history of Brasil, dating from earliest colonial times up until the proclamation of the Republic. There is also a very interesting collection of carriages from the XIX century, some historical paintings and the original letter written by D. Pedro II announcing the end of the Empire.
The Museum of the Republic is placed in one of

the most beautiful buildings in Rio, the Palace of Catete, built in 1866 by a German architect. From 1896 it served as the Presidential home until Getulio Vargas killed himself in 1954. In its rooms is exhibited an important collection of documents relating all the Presidents of the Republic.
The National Museum of Art, an imposing building built early this century, offers an excellent collection of Brazilian painting. Among the most famous works are pictures by Eliseu, Visconti, Presciliano Silva, Tarsila do

COOL DRINKS PEDDLER - IPANEMA BEACH

COOL DRINKS PEDDLER - LEBLON BEACH

SOFT DRINKS PEDDLER - IPANEMA BEACH

Amaral and Portinari.
For those wishing to learn more details of the history of Rio, a visit to the «City Museum» is recomended. This is located in the peaceful surroundings of the «City Park». A visit to the «Theatre Museum» is also recomended where to admire its faithful historical reconstruction of the world of show business.
In the Museum of Modern Art there are interesting collections and works by such famous artists as Picasso, Dalí and Matisse, together with works by contemporary Brazilians. There is also a wonderful selection of popular Brazilian music in the Museum of Sound and Image.
For those interested in History and Ethnology, there are two interesting museums, the Marine Museum and the Museum of the Indian, the latter with a comprehensive exhibition of the Brazilian indian culture.

SURFING
AT
ARPOADOR
BEACH

THE CARNIVAL

Nothing could sum up the history of Rio with so much wit as the popular «marchinha» which says that Brasil was born on April 21st, «two months after the Carnival». February is a historical landmark in Brazilian life for this is the traditional month for the celebration of the Carnival, although it may sometimes be held in March. All the carioca vitality explodes and overflows during the days of the Carnival. The samba starts in the popular neighborhoods and from there spreads all over the city.

The Carnival has its origin in the old celebration of the «entrudo» which the portuguese imported from the Azores. In those times the fiesta was a noisy orgy, often ending in violent riots. Then the Carnival became a celebration exclusive to the middle class until the XIX century when the first popular fancy dress dances were held. They were gay but without the animation of the commonfolk. It was the colored people with their dances and rites who brought life and soul to the carioca Carnival. Carnival societies and samba schools were founded, and since 1917 the samba has lent its rhythms and compass to the Carnival.

This festival of joy and free expression which breaks the monotony of city life is not merely an entertainment for it provides work to hundreds of people in the workshops where the dresses and trimming, masks and necklaces are

PRESIDENTE COSTA E SILVA BRIDGE OVER GUANABARA BAY

made. The Carnival is also a source of inspiration and enthusiasm for the popular artists, and offers an opportunity for everyone to express their creativeness and imagination. During these days of freedom and delirium, many romances are born, and others, not so strong break down under the strain of such a trial. At Carnival time, life is totally transformed, for this is above all a festival of rebirth.

A famous black composer of the thirties created the first samba school, known as «Deixa falar» («Let us talk»). Since then, these schools have grown and multiplied, and today they contribute a large parade which is one of the biggest attractions of the Carnival. At the sunday parades during the Carnival, more than 40,000 masquerade groups march through the avenues of the city singing and dancing in the most extravagant and fanciful manner. Excited people watch the parades from their semicircular seats. There is an intense competition among the samba schools to

RODRIGO DE FREITAS LAGOON

LAGOON IN THE BACKGROUND, IPANEMA AND LEBLON BEACHES

decide which offers most luxury and beauty, and each group presents a samba specially composed for the ocassion, with themes related to facts or figures from history, mythology or life in Rio.

There is no show on earth which can compare to the sunday parade of the samba schools in the Carnival. The «front paraders», who are old timers, open up the parade. Righ after them come the «Mestre sala» (Grand master) and the flag bearer, displaying the emblems and banner of the first school. Then comes the main section, formed by interminable rows of step and acrobatic dancers respectively, with their complicated movements, all moving forward in formation at a rhytmical compass, and playing tricks with the colors of their respective schools. The beat is marked by percussion, made up of hundreds of drummers with such typical instruments as little drums, «cuicas». etc.

JOCKEY CLUB

The Samba Schools form the base of the carioca Carnival. Some of them, (Mangueira, Portela, Salgueiro) for instance, already have a legendary history, and each school has its own symbols and followers. Mangueira shows greens and pinks, Portela blue and white, Salgueira red and blue, and so on and so forth. One of the best entertainments in Rio, apart from the Carnival, are the rehearsals of these schools, which are open to the public from september on.

The *bossa-nova* is an up-dated variety of the

LAGE PARK

LAGE PARK

BOTANICAL GARDEN

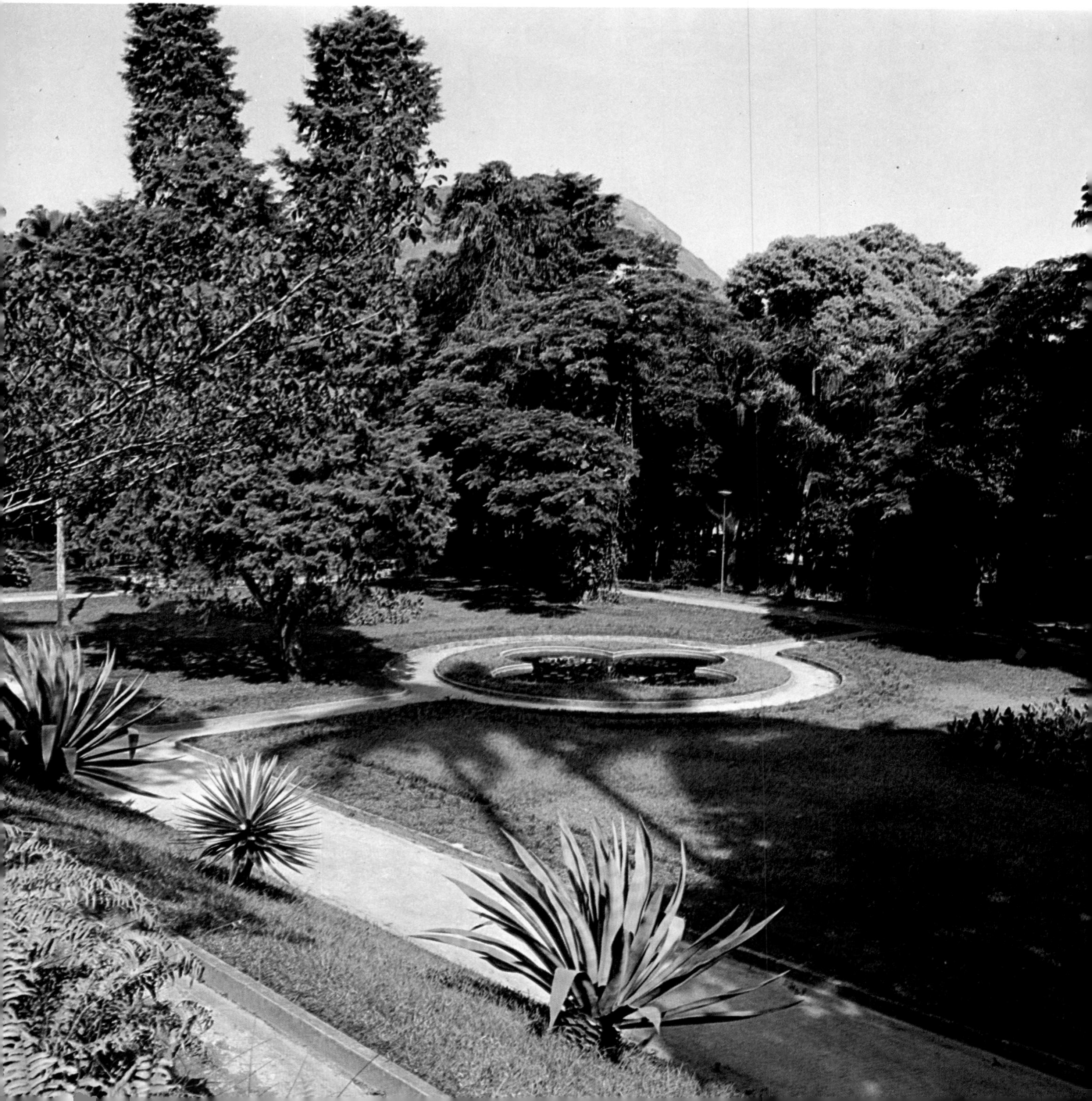

GUANABARA PALACE GARDENS

traditional samba. Today it is perhaps. one of the most popular rhythms in the world, and is a clear example of the ability of Brazilian music to renew itself without losing its poetry and singular rhythm.

When the Carnival comes to an end the whole city seems to sink into a state of melancholy.

Those who took part. extremely tired, even fall asleep in the streets. The dream is over for the poor who became the princes of that happy kingdom. The samba «Felicidade» (Happiness) expresses this post-Carnival feeling in a very poetic way when it says:

*BOTANICAL
GARDEN*

NATIONAL MUSEUM

«Tristeza nâo tem fim...
Felicidade sim!»

(Sadness never ends, only happiness does!).

This sadness, however, is poetical, sweet and human, and somehow the festival in Rio never comes to an end. Any event, (a victory of their football team, a New Year's celebration) is an excuse to have a small Carnival. The lively spirit of the cariocas knows no bounds.

NIGHTS OF RIO

Copacabana, Ipanema, Leblon, (Barra too, on weekends) are the most important centers of night-life with nights alive with samba rhythms gathering up all the happy bohemians. The carioca nightclubs present the most elegant and luxurious shows all year round, enlivened by the incomparable sensuality of the Brazilian women.

67

Young people, as a rule, prefer the atmosphere of the discoteques, where darkness and music are blended at maximum intensity.

Meanwhile, in the bars in the southern part of Rio people drink iced *chope* out in the open, sharing an unconventional and happy comradeship.

For those who prefer the cinema, a theater or a concert, there are several places in which to enjoy a spectacle of their choice, and they are sure to find wonderful samples of **Brazilian** folklore too.

Brazilian night-life has been since 1940, without interruption, an international attraction. In the early days the lights of the city around the famous «Cinelandia» and the street of El Passeio were already an attraction, and from there the gaiety extended into the avenues of Copacabana, and even as far as the residential district in the south. Today the happy night-life has invaded every corner of the city. The cariocas are chatting and dancing everywhere, on the terraces of São Conrado, in the hotel clubs, in the discoteques of Copacabana, and outside and inside of the famous Samba Schools where an eternal Carnival is always in motion. At the rehearsals of these schools we shall be able to meet Rio's «Queen of the night»: the mulatto girl, a perfect product of the blending of the races, living in a country where prejudice based on skin color is unknown.

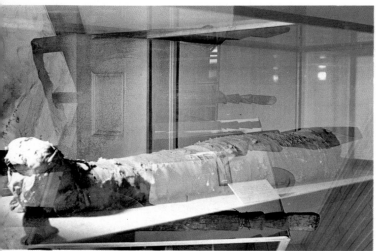

CARIOCA KITCHEN

The **Brazilian** food suits all tastes. The traveller will find a favorite dish on the menu of any restaurant in the city. For those who are fond of good meat the churrasquerias is their place, where food is eaten to the beat of live music. There are also many restaurants where dishes from different parts of Brasil are served.

NATIONAL MUSEUM - QUINTA DA BOAVISTA

VISTA CHINESA (CHINESA VIEW)

The Brazilian cuisine, like the history of the country, is a result of the blend of three different races: the indian, the black and the european. From this mixture has come a spicy and varied kind of food with infinite tastes and specialties. The food in the northern part of Brasil has the characteristic flavor of the native food. The dishes from Bahia use afro-brazilian condiments and spices. In the central part of the country one can feel the influence of the bandeirantes, those early adventurers who travelled around the country looking for gold and precious stones. In the south the typical dish is the churrasco, which is part of the daily

staple of the gauchos and cowboys of that region.

But the *feijoada* is, definitely, the most typical dish of the Brazilian cooking, consisting of black beans with chunks of pork. In the city, however, the tourist will find all the specialties of international cuisine ranging from French to Chinese, Potuguese, Spanish, German, etc... The exquisite tropical fruits should not be forgotten either: coconuts, bananas, pineapples, avocados, and countless juicy fruits from which delicious juices and shakes are made.

Besides the traditional restaurants, such as the Confiteria Colombo, we will find more refined and expensive places such as the Concorde, Michele, Mario's, Nino's etc., plus some others situated by the seashore or on the top of the mountains, always surrounded by the luxuriant freshness of this tropical garden.

SANTA TERESA TRAM

PEDRA DA GAVEA
(THE GAVEA ROCK)

SÃO CONRADO BEACH

MARACANA

The stadium of Mario Filho, better known as Maracaná, is a huge cement construction seating 200.000 spectators, which is the finest and most renowned stadium in the world. From 1948 until 1950, 11.000 workers worked in a race against time in order to make this dream come true. The 500.000 cement bags used for its construction would measure more —if piled up together— than the Empire State building, or would be enough to make a street a mile and a

MAYRINCK CHAPEL IN THE TIJUCA FOREST SMALL CASCADE

MARIO
FILHO
(MARA-
CANA)
STADIUM

MULATTO
GIRLS
OF
OBA-OBA
NIGHT-CLUB

SAMBA SCHOOL PARADE, THE GREAT ATTRACTION OF CARNIVAL.

BLACK MAGIC RITUALS.

half long. With the 180.000 cubic feet of stone that form its structure, a piramid 9,000 feet high could be built.

Maracaná is almost a city, with its 46 bars, its restaurants, apartments, first-aid centers and dressing rooms.

The Maracaná has witnessed the most important moments in the history of football and it was here that Pelé scored his 1.000th goal, an achievement never equalled by any other football player in the world.

Football is the Brazilian sport par excellence. Some of the teams which play in the national championships are known worldwide... Flamengo, Botafogo, Fluminense, Americo, Vasco de Gama, etc. All Brazilian are familiar

BLACK MAGIC RITUALS.

with the names of Pelé, Garrincha, Didí, Jairizinho and many others who play in the various Brazilian football teams. They are the real idols of the people.
The most famous political figures have passed through its doors: H. M. Queen Elizabeth of England, the Sha of Iran, Robert Kennedy. Kennedy even broke protocol when in a moment of elation he embraced Pelé under the shower in the dressing room after a game.
Over 25 years of existence, the Maracaná stadium has already welcomed 70 million

spectators, and has been the stage for the joy or dissapointment of the fans. In 1950 the defeat of the Brazilian selection against Uruguay was almost a national tragedy. But after this failure came the great victories of Brazilian football, the winning of the World championship in 1958, 1962 and 1970.

In Maracaná there is also an interesting Sports Museum, housing photographies and trophies of all the sports practiced in the country. Right beside it is the gimnasium «Gilberto Cardoso» better known as the «Maracaizinho» (little Maracaná), which is a large covered stadium with a capacity for 18.000 spectators.

NEW INTERNATIONAL AIRPORT - RIO DE JANEIRO

PAQUETA AND THE GUANABARA BAY

A visit to Rio is not complete without a visit to the ocean. At only a few minutes distance from the city and situated at one extreme of the Bay of Guanabara, lies the island of Paquetá, a refuge of solitude and calm.

Automobile traffic being forbidden, the island rests in a gentle twilight like a forgotten paradise. Its paths can be calmly travelled at the slow pace of an old tilbury, just as princes of yesterday did.

RIO IS IN THE CENTER OF THE BRAZILIAN JOWELRY INDUSTRY. IN THIS PAGE, SOME EXAMPLES OF BRAZILIAN SEMI-PRECIOUS STONES.

BLACK BEANS, (FEIJOADA), A REGIONAL DISH

Its beaches attract many bathers, while other people prefer to rent a bycicle and pedal their way over the pretty lanes which cross the island.

At night when the excursionists leave the beaches, Paquetá recovers its deep and poetical loneliness. The visitor can sleep at one of the local hotels and enjoy the quiet night in the midst of this garden still untouched by man. The trip to Paquetá offers us an opportunity to delight our eyes with the wonderful landscapes of the Bay of Guanabara. On one side, the beaches of Rio, Flamengo and Botafogo, on the other, the shore of Niteroi, with its beaches Gragoatá, Icaraí, Saco de Sâo Francisco, Jurujuba and Adâo y Eva, (Adam and Eve). Encircled by the rugged outlines of the Pâo de Azucar and the peak of Santa Cruz, the Bay of Guanabara stretches out over an area of 160 square miles. Connecting Rio and Niteroi is the famous bridge, a masterpiece of engineering, linking the two shores of the most beautiful bay in the whole world.

INDEX

Printed in Spain  GEOCOLOR®

COGRAF, S.A. Dep. Leg. - B - 38.372 - 79